M000018445

This journal belongs to

You'll learn more about a road by traveling it than by consulting all the maps in the world.

May your footsteps set you upon a lifetime journey of love.
May you wake each day with His blessings and sleep each night in His keeping.
And may you always walk in His tender care.

Isn't it splendid to think of all the things there are to find out about? It just makes me feel glad to be alive—it's such an interesting world.

Lucy Maud Montgomery

It is God to whom and with whom we travel,
and while He is the end of our journey,
He is also at every stopping place.

Elisabeth Elliot

He protected us on our entire journey and among
all the nations through which we traveled.

The Bible

No one realizes how beautiful it is to travel until he comes home and rests his head on his old, familiar pillow.

Lin Yutang

We may run, walk, stumble, drive, or fly, but let us never lose sight of the reason for the journey, or miss a chance to see a rainbow on the way.

Gloria Gaither

Rest is not idleness, and to lie sometimes on the grass under the trees on a summer's day, listening to the murmur of water...is by no means a waste of time.

Sir John Lubbock

I am with you and will watch over you wherever you go.

The Bible

The use of traveling is to regulate imagination by reality, and instead of thinking how things may be, to see them as they are.

Samuel Johnson

Only those who will risk going too far can possibly find out how far one can go.
T. S. Eliot

Each morning is the open door to a new world—new vistas, new aims, new tryings.

Leigh Mitchell Hodges

Go in peace. The presence of the LORD be with you on your way.

The Bible

*Each of us may be sure that if God sends us on stony paths
He will provide us with strong shoes.*

Alexander Maclaren

Happiness is not a station you arrive at, but a manner of traveling.

Margaret Lee Runbeck

Go forth seeking adventure. Open your eyes, your ears, your mind, your heart, your spirit and you'll find adventure everywhere.

Wilferd A. Peterson

Show me the right path, O LORD; point out the road for me to follow.

The Bible

$\mathscr{L}$ife is not a journey to the grave with the intention of arriving safely in one pretty and well preserved piece, but to skid across the line broadside, thoroughly used up, worn out, leaking oil, shouting GERONIMO!

Bill McKenna

Life is short and we never have enough time for gladdening the hearts of those who travel the way with us. O, be swift to love! Make haste to be kind.

Henri Frédéric Amiel

At every crossroad, follow your dream.
It is courageous to let your heart lead the way.

Thomas Leland

He refreshes my soul. He guides me along the right paths for his name's sake.

The Bible

They travel lightly whom God's grace carries.

Thomas à Kempis

*Every now and then go away, have a little relaxation.
For when you come back to your work, your judgment will be surer.*

Leonardo da Vinci

Discoveries are often made by...going off the main road, by trying the untried.

Frank Tyger

*P*ut your hope in the LORD. Travel steadily along his path.

The Bible

Today is your day! Your mountain is waiting. So...get on your way.

Theodor Seuss Geisel (Dr. Seuss)

The longer I live, the more my mind dwells upon the beauty and the wonder of the world.

John Burroughs

God wanted to join us on the road, to listen to our story, and to help us realize that we are not walking in circles but moving toward the house of peace and joy.

Henri J. M. Nouwen

The LORD bless you, and keep you;
the LORD make His face shine on you,
and be gracious to you.

The Bible

May the road rise to meet you, may the wind be always at your back...
And, until we meet again, may God hold you in the palm of His hand.

Irish Blessing

Ellie Claire® Gift & Paper Expressions
Franklin, TN 37067
EllieClaire.com
Ellie Claire is a registered trademark of Worthy Media, Inc.

See the World Travel Journal
© 2016 by Ellie Claire
Published by Ellie Claire, an imprint of Worthy Publishing Group,
a division of Worthy Media, Inc.

ISBN 978-1-63326-118-1

Stock or custom editions of Ellie Claire titles may be purchased in bulk for educational,
business, ministry, fundraising, or sales promotional use. For information, please e-mail
info@EllieClaire.com

Cover art © Shutterstock | www.shutterstock.com
Printed in China

5 6 7 8 9 10 11 12 13 – 23 22 21 20 19 18